The Lawrences

The Lawrences

Nathaniel Harris

ILLUSTRATED BY ANDREW FARMER

J M DENT & SONS LTD

First published 1976

Printed and bound in Great Britain by
Morrison & Gibb Ltd., London and Edinburgh
for J. M. Dent & Sons Ltd
Aldine House . Albemarle Street . London

This book is set in 11 on 12 pt Baskerville

ISBN 0 460 06677 3

Contents

Illustrations

A family group

The one photograph of the whole Lawrence family is a formal studio picture, taken in about 1894 or '95. It is not very good, even by the standards of the time. The faces of the sitters are rather blurred, and half of them seem to have been taken by surprise; at any rate the girls are staring gormlessly at the camera with their mouths hanging open, and brother Ernest in the back row is looking hard at something off to his right.

Still, the picture evidently satisfied the Lawrences, who put it on display over their parlour mantelpiece. It did the main job that Mr and Mrs Lawrence required of it: it presented a favourable, 'Sunday best' version of the family for the benefit of outsiders and of posterity. There was Arthur Lawrence, a typical powerful-looking Victorian father, dark-suited, massively bearded, with a flower in his button-hole and a watch chain peeping out of his waistcoat. He looked a little uncomfortable with his fists balanced awkwardly on his thighs, but no one would be likely to guess that he came home black every night from working at the pit, or that he preferred the public bar to family life. Or that his fine upstanding sons and daughters, grouped round their parents, hated him as much as they worshipped their mother.

Only Mrs Lawrence's appearance causes some surprise: six years younger than her husband, she could easily pass as his mother. The miner is hale and hearty; the housewife looks worn down with work. Her hair is scraped tightly back, accentuating the smallness of her head; the blurred, irregular little features contrast forcibly with the apparent strength of her husband's face. Mrs Lawrence's face, and her tiny hands, are the only parts of her body that can be seen: all the rest is covered by a voluminous, shapeless black dress that helps to make her look old and pathetic.

The camera lied here as well, or at least in part: Lydia Lawrence was a sharp, tough little woman, quite capable of holding her own against her husband. It lied about Ernest too: the heavy-faced, rather brutal-looking young man was quick and gay and clever—more so than his amiable elder brother, George, a young man of film-star

The Lawrence family at the photographer's

good looks, though a head shorter than Ernest. Aged about nineteen and seventeen, the brothers had lived and worked away from home for some time, so the photograph must have been taken during one of the family's reunions. The group is completed by the younger children, who face the camera with blankly stupid expressions. Emily was about thirteen; Bert, with a bow tie and big white collar turned down over his jacket, was three years younger; and Ada, at about eight, still has her hair in ringlets.

The photographic 'Sunday best' version of the Lawrences might be the only one left, if little Bert had not gone on to become a writer. As a man he re-created his childhood experiences in novels, stories and plays; and because he became famous, his friends and relatives also put down their memories of that time. So there is a quantity of information available about this particular mining family, though in their day they were no different from any of the others who struggled along in the little Nottinghamshire mining town of Eastwood. With this information we can build up a picture of the life, work and surroundings of the Lawrence family in the later years of the nineteenth-century—beginning with a meeting and a marriage in the city of Nottingham.

Love and marriage

Lydia Beardsall met Arthur Lawrence in the winter of 1874-5, fell in love with him, and married him two days after Christmas 1875.

The Beardsalls were a Derbyshire family who had moved across the county boundary to Nottingham, drawn there by the booming lace industry. Lydia's grandfather made a fortune as a lace manufacturer, and then lost it in a slump—a not unusual event in the early 'roller-coaster' phase of the Industrial Revolution. His son, George Beardsall, though brought up in poverty, became an engineer—an admittedly elastic term, used by the Victorians to describe almost anybody who understood the workings of some kind of machinery. At first George Beardsall worked for a firm of Nottingham carriage-makers; later, after marrying, he moved to Sheerness in Kent, where he became a foreman in the dockyards. Although he raised a sizeable family, he seems to have been a cold, capable man who poured most of his emotions into religion. He quarrelled about it with two of the most distinguished Nottingham men of his time, Jesse Boot the chemist and William Booth the Salvationist, and made a name for himself as a lay preacher in the Wesleyan Methodist chapel at Sheerness.

George Beardsall could be roughly described as lower middle class. In practical terms this meant that he didn't do heavy work with his hands; he dressed and behaved in a serious and decent manner (not, for example shouting, fighting, swearing, or getting drunk in public); saved his money; and brought up his sons to be like himself, and his daughters to be refined, 'thinking' young women. Whether you called them ladies and gentlemen would depend on whether you viewed them from above or below. The older definition of gentility in terms of birth, breeding and money was certainly giving way to the more moralistic Victorian idea of a gentleman (or lady) as a refined, truthful, good-mannered person; so perhaps we can give the Beardsalls the benefit of the doubt. At the same time they were not so elevated that they could not slip right out of the 'respectable' classes (like one of Lydia's brothers, a scapegrace whose many dubious ventures included running a public house—something no

12

man could possibly do in the Victorian era and still call himself a gentleman).

Lydia was emphatically a 'refined, thinking person'. She seems to have lacked conventional, 'ladylike' accomplishments such as playing the piano and painting watercolours, but she wrote poetry which she submitted to magazines (unsuccessfully) and is said to have written entertaining letters in an elegant hand. She was reasonably well educated, had assisted the teacher in a little private school for a while, and loved reading and talking about 'ideas'—though it seems unlikely that the ideas went far beyond Nonconformist notions of life, art and morals.

To Arthur Lawrence, who had spent most of his life among colliers and their womenfolk, Lydia must have seemed very much a 'lady'. At the same time there was no great gulf between them, for they were relatives by marriage: Arthur's aunt had married Lydia's uncle, and it was at their house that the young couple first met.

They were oddly matched. Arthur Lawrence was a skilled workman; he had been called on a temporary basis to Nottingham, leaving his home in the village of Brinsley, a few kilometres away, to help sink a new mine-shaft at Clifton. But all the same he was a miner, condemned to pit-dirt, though he told Lydia that he was a 'contractor'—a statement that was technically correct but totally misleading. He could read—but only newspapers, with considerable labour. He had no interest in ideas, or even any conception that they might be of passionate concern to some people. And he spoke a broad dialect that made the greatest possible contrast to Lydia's crisp, correct speech.

So what brought them together? It is easy to understand the collier being attracted by a delicate, refined, ladylike creature: Lydia's qualities were not only socially superior, but also those of the Victorian womanly ideal. But what drew *her* to Arthur Lawrence? The simple and obvious answer is sex appeal. Lawrence was well built, with a ruddy complexion, red lips and full dark beard and moustache covering a face that had never (he boasted) known a razor. Above all, Arthur Lawrence had warmth and physical vitality. Lydia despised frivolous pursuits such as dancing, but there was no doubt that Lawrence was a wonderful dancer—so good that he had even held classes in his native Brinsley. His great physical presence and caressing 'thees' and 'thous' may have appealed to Lydia all the more because she had once been jilted by a young man as 'refined' as

13

herself—which had not prevented him from marrying his landlady for her money; she probably confused Arthur Lawrence's spontaneity with sincerity.

Finally there was the prospect—dear to the female Victorian heart—of purifying and ennobling her man. For like most miners in those days, Arthur Lawrence looked on the pub as a second home; whereas Lydia, like so many Nonconformists, looked on it as a stopping-place on the road to perdition. Infatuated with Lydia, Arthur Lawrence willingly allowed himself to be saved: he 'signed the pledge' and renounced 'the demon drink'.

But however strong the pull of sex, the courtship proceeded with decorum, and Arthur and Lydia were not married until they had known each other for about a year. The ceremony took place at St Stephen's, the parish church of Sneinton. The village was connected with the Beardsalls, not the Lawrences, so it must have been Lydia the Methodist who chose to be married by a Church of England clergyman. (We shall find this seeming indifference to denominations appearing again later on.)

On the marriage licence Arthur Lawrence is described as a 'mining contractor'.

There is a story that on the first day Arthur Lawrence came home from the pit to his new wife, she thought a Negro had broken into the house: she refused to believe that this man with the blackened face, red lips and brilliant white eyeballs could be her 'contractor' husband.

It's a good story, but not very likely to be true. Even if Arthur Lawrence had romanced a bit about his job, Lydia must have acquired some idea of mining life in advance, if only from common observation. What is more likely is that she had known what it would be like in a general sort of way, but had not made the imaginative effort needed to visualize the reality as and when it applied to her. After all, when she saw him during their courting days, Arthur was always clean and smart in his best suit. Now, all at once, Lydia was faced with a black, weary creature who hung up his pit-coat, briefly washed his hands, and slumped down before the kitchen table, waiting for his dinner. His head, shoulders and arms were still begrimed, and his thick flannel singlet was caked with pit-dust.

Lydia Lawrence found out—if she did not already know—that

14

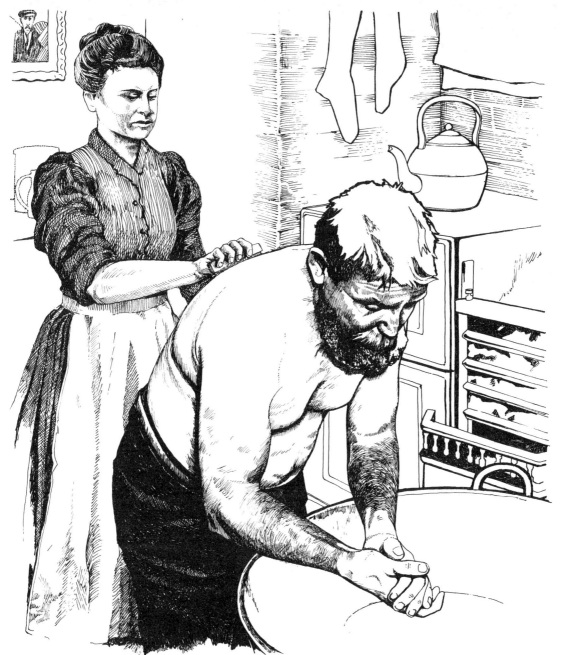

A miner's wife scrubs her husband

every collier behaved like this. They all said they were too tired to wash thoroughly before they had eaten; and it was true. After dinner they expected their wives to heat water for them in a boiler and pour it into a tub or bucket. Then the miner stripped to the waist and washed himself; his wife had to scrub the coal-dust off his back—not the sort of thing a well-brought-up young lady expected to do, although since there was nobody else available she had no choice.

Lydia learned to cope with it all, and to get on with the other men's wives (though her neighbours always thought her a bit stuck-up). But it was a come-down for her, and from this time onwards she had a grievance against life. She was lonely for the kind of 'intellectual' company she had known, and she felt wasted and—as the children came—trapped.

But first there was the business of settling down. Early in their marriage the Lawrences lived in several little towns in the Nottingham mining country. For a time they stayed at Brinsley, the village where Arthur Lawrence had been born, and where he had worked down the pit since boyhood. Finally they moved down the road to Eastwood, which was to be their home for over thirty years.

Eastwood

Eastwood was (and is) just inside Nottinghamshire, set among hills from which it looks down on the narrow little Erewash Valley; the Erewash, hardly more than a stream, is the boundary between Nottinghamshire and Derbyshire. The town consisted of shops and buildings strung out along the hilltop on the Nottingham Road, going in a roughly east-west direction. Below the road, on a slope running down towards the north, were the blocks of dull red-brick miners' houses. At the western end of the town was the market place, where the roads to Nottingham, Mansfield, Derby and Ilkeston all met; Brinsley, where Arthur Lawrence carried on working after the move to Eastwood, was on the Mansfield Road, just to the north.

Eastwood was a direct product of the Industrial Revolution. At the end of the eighteenth century about a hundred people lived there; by the end of the nineteenth there were well over four thousand, drawn to the town directly or indirectly by the nearby mines. For the Industrial Revolution was, more than anything else, an energy revolution; and the fuel that created almost all the energy was coal. It drove steam engines, smelted iron, and kept a rapidly growing population warm in winter. And so the shallow diggings of past centuries were transformed into great industrial enterprises, and the vastly increased production of the mines around Nottingham was transported—mainly to the Leicester area—by barges on the Erewash Canal, built in the 1770s. After 1830 the prosperity of the mines was threatened by the development of the railway network north of Leicester. The coal from that area now became cheaper than Nottinghamshire coal; so the Nottinghamshire magnates became the driving force behind a scheme to build a railway that would make *their* coal quick and cheap to transport, and give them a chance to recapture the lost market. In 1832 a great meeting was held at the Sun Inn, on the crossroads at Eastwood, and from this developed one of the greatest British railway companies, the Midland. Chains of events like this make sense of the well-known generalizations about the Industrial Revolution: we can see the connections between coal and steam, canals and railways, industry and the growth of towns.

17

Nottingham Road, Eastwood

In the course of the nineteenth-century, Eastwood became the market town serving the surrounding countryside, and also the half a dozen nearby collieries. It also became a 'company town', dominated by the mine-owners Barber, Walker and Co. They were among the chief subscribers to the 'Erewash Valley Railway Company'—the first name for the railway planned at the Sun Inn meeting. And the firm also built blocks of miners' dwellings below Nottingham Road, gaining additional power by being at once landlord and employer.

In typical English fashion, both Barbers and Walkers used the money they made from coal to build up country estates, which meant that they were not mere capitalists but also gentry—members of the traditional class of 'squires' and magistrates, still regarded as the backbone of England. Furthermore, they were able to maintain huge estates very near the collieries they owned: the Walkers around their mansion at Eastwood Hall, on the Mansfield Road between Eastwood and Brinsley, and the Barbers around Lamb Close, over to the north-east. For although industrialized, Eastwood was no urban giant like Birmingham or the pottery towns, blotting out every trace of nature. The town and the collieries were small scars on a still-lovely landscape. After a few minutes' walk down from the Nottingham Road, you could cross Beauvale Brook and go on into the lanes and paths of a valley filled with small farms and even a few patches of woodland left over from the old Sherwood Forest.

So the colliers who lived on that slope were thoroughly at home in the countryside; they walked through it every morning to work, and might even, like Arthur Lawrence, take time out to pick mushrooms or scoop up an abandoned baby rabbit. And their children—including the Lawrence children—had an interesting, mixed inheritance that made them as familiar with flowers and streams as with ashpits and railways.

The Lawrences' first Eastwood home was in Victoria Street, one of the turnings off the Nottingham Road, not far from the market place. The little red-brick house was on the corner of an undistinguished terrace, standing upright at a sharp angle to the steeply falling road. But it was certainly nothing to be ashamed of, for although the street door opened directly on to the front room, the house itself was surprisingly roomy and substantial. The large rectangular ground-floor window gave Lydia Lawrence the idea that the front room might be turned into a shop, and for a while she displayed lace goods for sale. But either the 'shop' was a failure, or her growing family started to take up all her time. The lace business was abandoned, and Lydia reconciled herself to being a simple collier's wife.

She was certainly not happy in the role, and her sense of grievance was strengthened by Arthur Lawrence's behaviour. For a time he had happily flourished the teetotaller's blue ribbon, but soon he began to stop off at the pub before coming home. When Mrs Lawrence nagged him, or treated him with the icy contempt that comes easily to the better-educated and stone-cold sober, he raged, banged the table, and occasionally hit her. And, as often as he could afford it, he stayed out all evening at the pub.

At this distance we can feel sorry for both of them. Mrs Lawrence was held fast in a poor, dirty, narrow life, with a man whose behaviour disgusted her, and who had no conception of the ideas and delicacies that meant a good deal to her. Arthur Lawrence slaved underground to keep a wife who made him feel small—and that in a community where the breadwinner was supposed to be 'th' mester' (the master), to be obeyed and waited on when he came home from the pit. Instead, Arthur's harmless convivial drinking had been denounced as disgusting and sinful by his rigidly puritanical spouse; in effect he had been driven from the home he worked to maintain—driven to spend more instead of less time at the pub.

There is not much point in taking sides: the Lawrences were just hopelessly mismatched. And it was a tragedy in the nineteenth-century style, without a violent or dramatic ending: husband and wife, tied together for life by convention, by shared poverty, and soon by children.

Mrs Lawrence had five children within eleven years: a fair but not outstanding score in an age when big families were normal, and the only form of birth control available to the working class was 'self-discipline', often confidently recommended by the better-off who did not need to resort to it. In the case of the Lawrences, quarrelling may have acted as a contraceptive, abetted by the effects of alcohol and fatigue on Mr Lawrence. At any rate, after the arrival of George in 1876 and Ernest in 1878, there was a gap until the birth of Emily in 1882. David Herbert—'Bert'—followed in 1885, and Ada in 1887. After that, though Mrs Lawrence was still only in her mid-thirties, there were no more children.

It was just as well, for in the early years it was evidently a struggle to make ends meet. The clearest sign of it was the sacrifice of one of

'The Squares'

the children. When Lydia Lawrence fell ill, George, her eldest child, spent a year at Sneinton, with his great-grandfather John Newton. (The eighty-year-old Newton, Lydia's maternal grandfather, was a retired lace-factory hand, and was also well known as a composer of Nonconformist hymns.) And by 1887—perhaps because Lydia was expecting yet another child—George had left home for good, going to Nottingham as an apprentice picture-framer in his uncle's shop.

As in many other families, the older Lawrence children no doubt had to look after the younger ones, and passed down the clothes they had outgrown. Sheer momentum must have taken them all down Victoria Street to play in 'the Squares'. These were prime examples of the crude, ugly buildings put up for working people in the nineteenth-century—although there were still-worse places, even in Eastwood. Here were rows of mean little four-room houses, and, at the back of them, rows of box-like back yards and ashpits forming squares around two large, uneven patches of earth. On these the colliers' wives hung out their washing on their clothes-lines and the children played in noisy gangs.

Soon after the birth of Ada in 1887, the Lawrences and their children moved down past the Squares to a new home. This was right on the edge of town, in a group of eight blocks known as the Breach. Like the Squares, they were terrace houses put up by Barber, Walker and Co., but they were more recent and larger, with little gardens fronting the street, attics with dormer windows standing up from the slate roofs, and long back gardens leading down to the privy and ashpits. Among the mining folk, who were as intensely class-conscious as other Victorians, the Breach was regarded as much less 'common' than the Squares. And the Lawrences' house was a cut above the others on their row, because it was an end house and the family paid sixpence a week more rent than other people—five shillings and sixpence instead of five shillings. The practical advantage of being at the end of the row was that there were three clear sides of the house with windows, letting a lot more light into the interior; and the Lawrences had an extra strip of ground linking the front and back gardens. There was also a certain prestige in the different siting of the house, which stood side on against the rest of the row, and with the shed-like porch set round to the left, facing the side garden.

Seen from the front, the rows making up the Breach were drab,

22

The Lawrences' house in the Breach

but solid and decent. Unfortunately the ground-floor front room was always fitted out as a parlour, which working-class families almost never used. It contained the best furniture (often including an upright piano), smelled of polish and lack of occupation, and was occasionally opened up on some formal occasion—to entertain strangers or lay out a body. The living room, and real centre of the house, was the kitchen—though for people in the Breach this meant living with a view on to the ashpits and privies, and the alley separating two rows of back gardens.

To some extent, then, squalor and ugliness were the fault of the inhabitants rather than the mineowner. Still, there is no denying that the Breach and all the other miners' dwellings in Eastwood were singularly unattractive. What should not be overlooked is that they were far superior to the buildings they replaced. In 1902 a ninety-three-year-old collier described the miners' cottages of his boyhood: they were thatched, *single-room* dwellings, probably more 'picturesque' than the Breach, but far more squalid and insanitary. When Barber, Walker and Co. put up these dull little red-brick rows, they were performing an important public service; and the rows are still there today, mostly in good condition—a tribute to the soundness of Victorian building, though their continued existence may not say much for twentieth-century housing programmes.

The kitchen at the Breach was comfortable, though crowded. There was a large fire always going in the fireplace, for the miners got their coal cheap and it was so hot down the pit that they tended to feel the slightest draught in a room. Cooking and hot water were provided by the cast-iron kitchen range, laid out like two black filing-cabinets, one on either side of the fire. One box was the oven, the other the boiler, both heated by the fire that kept the room warm—a remarkably economical arrangement in wintertime, but inconvenient and uncomfortable in summer. Above the fire itself, at the top of the grate, stood the hob, a ledge on which food could be fried and kettles boiled. Properly speaking the whole unit, including the fire, made up the kitchen range; and all of it, including the bars of the grate, had to be black-leaded. This was one of the most laborious of all household tasks, and involved the application to the metal of a substance like boot-polish, which was brushed hard until the iron was a brilliant shining black.

In the Lawrences' kitchen there was a rocking chair for Mrs

24

Miner's living room and kitchen

Lawrence on one side of the fire, and on the other side an armchair of the 'Windsor' type, with a sort of 'fan' pattern of spokes, reserved for Mr Lawrence. There were other chairs, cupboards and dressers, a large mahogany table on which the family ate their meals, a chintz-covered sofa, and a bookcase which filled up over the years with dictionaries, the children's calf-bound prize books, and *The World's Famous Literature*, a set bought by Ernest which became the family's most treasured possession. On the walls there were a few framed prints, mostly taken from magazines. The Lawrences' kitchen would probably strike us as more attractive than their neighbours' rooms, for Lydia Lawrence believed it was better to do without ornaments than to have cheap, tawdry ones. She was content with a pair of brass candlesticks on the mantelpiece and a vase of flowers somewhere in the room, whereas most ordinary people crammed their houses with a vast range of knick-knacks from pottery dogs to imitation fruit made of wax.

Just off from the kitchen was the scullery, a room hardly bigger than a cupboard, containing the cold-water tap and sink. Upstairs were the bedrooms, and above them the tiny attic. Outside the back door there was a coal-fired boiler and a water pump.

This, then, was the setting of family life in the Breach, where the Lawrences' house has now been made into a museum. Life was pretty much the same in all the houses the family rented. It was a struggle, but one that did secure the necessities of life and even a few cheap 'luxuries', like paints for the children. It is worth remembering that the Lawrences were never numbered among 'the Poor'—the Victorian term for the millions who always lived from hand to mouth, an entire family crowded into a single room, with no prospect but (sooner or later) ending in the workhouse. And there were still more degraded folk who survived by scavenging, or by trudging wearily from one 'spike' (dosshouse) to the next, as the American writer Jack London describes in *People of the Abyss*. Compared with these lost souls of the city, the 'respectable' working class were well-off, especially if they lived in a tight community like mining Eastwood, with strong traditions of mutual aid. Insurance and 'the compensation' (paid by the colliery company after accidents) provided a safety-net against disaster; and even in periods of short-time working nobody starved, though on at least one occasion Mrs Lawrence, handed fourteen shillings to manage on for the week, felt she could not go on and burst into tears.

Picking mushrooms on the way to work

In such times the family benefited from the fact that it was much more self-sufficient than was possible for big-city dwellers. Mr Lawrence mended the family's shoes, kettles and pans, hung up rows of herbs in the attic for Mrs Lawrence to make into the vaguely medicinal herb beer he loved, and sometimes brought home mushrooms picked on his early morning walk to work. The children scoured the countryside for blackberries so that their mother could make pies, and also gathered coltsfoot and mushrooms. Emily, the oldest girl, knitted gloves and stockings; her mother made such clothes as she could. And on Friday night after dinner, Mrs Lawrence baked her own bread in the oven, leaving one of the older children to watch over it while she went shopping in the market place.

There is much more to be said about life at home, but first let us look at the basis of it all: life underground at the coal face.

'Down pit'

A technical description of nineteenth-century mining would be out of place in a book centred on family life. But some aspects of the collier's working life do deserve attention, for they deeply influenced his personality and shaped the community he lived in.

We can begin with a negative statement: mining was essentially unmechanized, and remained so until long after Arthur Lawrence's time. The Industrial Revolution created an enormous demand for coal to power engines and machinery, but its impact on mining techniques was largely restricted to the engines that drove the ventilation fans and winding mechanisms. Winning coal from the earth still involved gangs of men hacking away at the coal face and loading the yield on to trucks, to be hauled away by horses. (The bad old days—when women and children worked underground—had long been over, though Arthur Lawrence claimed that he had gone to work at Brinsley at the age of seven. Some collieries had coal-cutters, driven by compressed air or electricity, to cut away the bottom of the seam, which was a necessary preliminary to the main attack on the coal face. But the machines were less effective than expected, and at Brinsley and most other collieries the work was done by hand. The man who did it—the 'holer'—had the hardest and dirtiest of all jobs in the mine: he worked lying down on his side, chipping away at the bottom of the coal face and eventually disappearing from sight under it. On the other hand, the use of explosives based on dynamite—employed with caution to loosen the rock—marked a great advance in safety over the crude gunpowder used a few years before. As a man Bert Lawrence recalled the delight with which he watched his father making fuses from wheatstraws, neatly cutting and packing them with gunpowder, and then sealing the ends with little pieces of soap.

Arthur Lawrence was a skilled, responsible man. He was a 'butty',

29

which meant that he was employed to take charge of a section of the coal-face, known as a 'stall'. He was paid by the week according to the amount of coal won from the stall, and he himself paid the two or three 'day men' who assisted him. So in a sense he was a 'contractor', as he had told Lydia Beardsall many years before. And it is true that as a butty he enjoyed a certain extra social standing: he could lord it a little over his day-men on a Friday night, at home or in the pub, while he shared out the week's earnings. But of course he was essentially a collier among colliers, both in the world's eyes and in his own: life 'down pit' developed an intense cameraderie that mattered more than any superficial distinctions.

This life was so hard and strange that it is almost impossible to get an imaginative hold on it. The modern miner's job is not easy, but the worst work is done by machinery, shifts are comparatively short, and at the end of the day the miner can relax and clean himself thoroughly and quickly at pithead baths. Arthur Lawrence arrived for work at six in the morning—unless he was on the night shift—and stayed underground until about four in the afternoon (to the envy of workers in other trades, whose hours were much longer!). He lunched at his stall on a couple of slices of bread and dripping and perhaps an apple; and at frequent intervals he wetted his dusty throat with cold tea from a tin bottle. Much of his life was lived by the dim light of a Davey safety lamp, or, if he was certain there was no gas lingering in the mine, by the brighter light of a candle; in winter he can never have seen daylight during many a working week.

Explosions caused by gas were the most dramatic hazards in a collier's life; there was a big though relatively harmless one at Brinsley in 1883, when the ventilation fans were turned off for the weekend, allowing gas to settle at the bottom of the mine. Hundreds might be killed in one of the great mine disasters—which was why the colliers reluctantly carried safety lamps, though they cursed their dimness: it made it hard to see what you were doing, and contributed to a strange occupational disease called nystagmus, which caused the eyeballs to oscillate wildly at the approach of light. But even more accidents were caused by roof falls; they generally involved only one or a few people, but they happened all the time. A crushed foot or a broken collarbone were everyday events, and the likelihood of spending an accident-free lifetime down the pit was nil. Even the possibility of being killed was statistically strong enough to be disturbing: more likely than being killed if you were a soldier in

'Down pit'

many nineteenth-century battles. From this point of view the miner's occupation was a unique one.

And then there was the sheer physical labour involved in the job, visible in the miner's overdeveloped arm and shoulder muscles—and in his dragging steps at the end of the day, especially noticeable once he was past first youth. One of the best accounts of what this was like is given in George Orwell's book *The Road to Wigan Pier*. Orwell describes the agonizing effects of travelling long distances underground, *stooping* almost all the way: he found that he was aching and exhausted, with a crick in his neck and pains in the knees and thighs, by the time he had reached the coal-face (anything from one-and-a-half to four kilometres from the bottom of the mine-shaft). And it was only at this point that the collier's working day began. For hours on end he was hacking or shovelling on his knees—which meant that the whole strain of the work was taken on his arms and shoulders (quite a different proposition from working standing up). The dust, heat, noise and confusion added up to the conventional idea of hell, an impression intensified by the lack of space and the consciousness of being trapped beneath a mountain of rock that was only held up by a few wooden props. At the end of the day the colliers came up to the surface in the cage (lift), their faces pale under their masks of coal, as a result of breathing foul air for many hours.

That was in the 1930s, when conditions were if anything better than in Arthur Lawrence's time. In view of the way their working lives were spent, it is hardly surprising that Lawrence and his fellow workers felt the need of lively pleasures—and that, if only for the want of anything else, meant the public house. They often justified their drinking on the grounds that mining was dry work, and that only beer effectively washed the coal-dust from their throats. But the truth was that the pub was the only social centre for ordinary people in any mining town.

And here the cameraderie of the pit was carried on into the evening and weekends. It was a virtually all-male society (for no respectable woman would go to a public house), a working-class equivalent to the all-male clubs of the upper classes. At other times too—during fairs, short-time working and strikes—the colliers tended to stay together. They pub-crawled through the countryside to Nottingham, or took the train into the city to watch a football match; and in bad times, when they had no money and no work, they would congregate together in groups in the streets and squares of Eastwood, squatting on their heels in a peculiarly characteristic way. For long periods of time Eastwood was like a racially divided community—the men with one way of life, and the women and children with another.

Occasions

Domestic life had its rituals too. After the evening round of dining, washing and visiting the public house, Mr Lawrence retired to bed. Mrs Lawrence put a big lump of coal on the fire so that it would last the night, laid out her husband's moleskin pit-trousers in front of it, and set the table for the morning. Then she turned off the gas and went to bed herself.

Mr Lawrence was up by five o'clock in the morning; everything was in readiness for him, so there was no need for his wife to get up. He got his own breakfast, and seems to have thoroughly enjoyed himself making tea and toasting bacon in front of the fire, letting the sizzling drops of fat drip down on to slices of bread. Then at dawn he went off through the fields to Brinsley colliery.

Mrs Lawrence also had a full and exhausting day before her—and one in some ways more demoralizing than her husband's, since she was a less sociable being. She cooked (and washed up) two meals a day, for she rightly believed that her children needed nourishment at midday. She mended and boiled and scrubbed and hung out the clothes of her family of six, including Arthur Lawrence's dust-caked singlets, neckerchieves and socks. She cleaned and tidied a house ravaged by children, and specked and smeared by coal-dust that tended to find its way everywhere. And she put on the bonnet and dark clothes she always wore, and trudged up to Nottingham Road for her shopping.

One of her main ports of call was 'the Co-op', already a great working-class institution that was particularly strong in the North and Midlands. The 'Rochdale Pioneers', a group of idealistic workingmen, had started the movement in 1844, opening a shop in Toad Lane, Rochdale. Business was conducted on a revolutionary but practical principle: the shop charged market prices but divided the profits among Co-op members in proportion to the amount they purchased. The movement boomed from the 'fifties, branched out into wholesaling in the 'seventies, and for a time looked like a viable general alternative to capitalism. It appealed to people like Mrs Lawrence, who had no time for Socialism—now reviving after long neglect—but believed in the virtues of hard work and self-help. And for the majority of working-class families, rarely able to save much, the dividend—'divi'—was a very useful windfall. The Lawrences used the shop so regularly that, years later, having travelled and lived in many parts of the world, Bert Lawrence claimed that he still remembered his Co-op number.

Friday was a special day. It still is for many people, and for the same reason: it is pay-day and the threshold to the weekend. Miners often sent their wives or children to collect their wages at the company offices, in a big house on the Mansfield Road, roughly opposite the Barbers' home at Eastwood Hall. School even closed a few minutes early on Friday afternoon so that the children could reach the offices in time. Each of Mrs Lawrence's sons in turn performed the errand when they were old enough, though the timid, sensitive Bert went through agonies when he was exposed to the banter of Mr Brenthall the cashier.

When Arthur Lawrence had come home, eaten, washed and dressed in everyday clothes, he would divide up the money with his daymen. If he did it at home, Mrs Lawrence would leave the kitchen, for a wife was not supposed to know how much her husband earned: that way she couldn't complain about the size of her share. Wages were likely to vary a great deal. As a butty, Arthur Lawrence might earn as much as five pounds in a really good week, though usually the sum must have been closer to two. Mrs Lawrence seems to have received an average of about thirty shillings (£1.50) a week for housekeeping, from which she paid the rent, trade union dues that Arthur would probably have been too careless to deal with regularly, and 'clubs' and other forms of welfare payment. As we have seen, the housekeeping money sustained life but left little to spare. Ironically, the various benefit payments, made when Mr Lawrence was in hospital as a result of an accident at the pit, often amounted to more than a normal week's housekeeping; so that the family hoped he would get better—but not too soon.

There were bad times too. Colliers were paid by the amount of coal they won; so if a stall proved poor—hard to work, or mixed up with great lumps of rock—their earnings could be very low. There is some evidence that Mr Lawrence's earnings fell over the years, either because he was getting older or because his independent attitude antagonized the white-collar overseers, so that they gave him the poorest stalls to work; like many men engaged in hard physical

35

labour he looked on clerical jobs as not really work at all, and made no secret of the fact.

Still, the week when Mrs Lawrence had to manage on fourteen shillings and five-pence-halfpenny was an exception. Most Friday nights, when she wandered among the covered stalls in front of the Sun Inn, she had ninepence or a shilling to spend on extras—a little bit of lace, a pretty dish or a few flowers. The tiny market place was thronged with women looking over goods and haggling; others crossed the road and stared at the fine clothes in George Cullen's impressive drapery store—clothes so absurdly out of place in Eastwood that the dandyish, ever-sanguine Cullen would eventually be forced to sell them for a fraction of their value.

The town was most alive at this time. The streets were full of men on their way to the pub, the billiard hall, or a sixpenny 'hop'; if they were not driven by the urgencies of courting they might linger for a while and give ear to an orator who had set up his soap-box near the market.

By eleven o'clock it was all over. The stalls had closed and the women left long before; all the respectable girls had reluctantly left their young men, or were just arriving home to a motherly scolding about the dangers of late-night passion and men inflamed with drink; the men themselves were walking, reeling or crawling home.

Saturday was less ritualized. For wives, of course, it was another working day, complicated by having the children home from school. And the house had to be kept spick-and-span over the weekend, ready to receive callers. It was a day for excursions and visits, though it might also be one for two long sessions at the pub, depending on finances and relations at home.

Sunday was different from every other day: it was dedicated almost entirely to rest and religion. Mrs Lawrence took her children morning and evening to the Congregationalist Chapel on the corner of the Nottingham Road and Albert Street, one turning down from Victoria Street. The children went to Sunday School as well, joined the Young People's Society of Christian Endeavour, and spent one evening a week at the anti-liquor Band of Hope, where they solemnly signed the abstainers' pledge and roared out 'There's a serpent in the glass, dash it down!' and other rousing songs. Mr Lawrence rarely attended chapel (though he made a good impression when he did), presumably finding small comfort in the temperance propaganda and rather self-consciously 'intellectual' atmosphere.

36

Eastwood market

It was probably just this atmosphere that attracted Mrs Lawrence. She was in deadly earnest about religion, and yet had twice changed the denomination to which she belonged, from Wesleyan Methodism to the Church of England, and from that to Congregationalism. It is possible that she experienced two serious changes of heart, but more likely that, like many other people, she found the differences between the 'Protestant' sects relatively unimportant. Church of England Evangelicals and Nonconformists had a good deal in common temperamentally and doctrinally, especially by contrast with the High Church Anglicans and the Roman Catholics, both increasingly active in England since the middle of the century; and in fact the Methodists and Congregationalists of Eastwood occasionally held joint functions. For most people, the differences between denominations were mainly a matter of tone or class. Mrs Lawrence would scarcely have been happy at the highly emotional, hell-and-damnation meetings of the Primitive Methodists, though many colliers were 'Prim Ranters' and their chapel on the Squares had largely been built by the miners themselves. Much the same was true of the Baptists; whereas Congregationalism had acquired a 'genteel' aura by the nineteenth-century, combined with a reserved fervour that appealed to respectable but hard-working people such as shopkeepers and smallholders. Such people believed in self-help and the virtues of independence; so that the Congregationalist system—which left every congregation free to choose its own forms of worship—had a deep attraction for them. In practice the minister did most of the choosing, but the conviction of participation and ultimate authority meant a good deal to Mrs Lawrence and other members of the flock.

The Congregationalists were the direct descendants of the Independents, who had briefly ruled England under the leadership of Oliver Cromwell, just over two centuries before. But by the nineteenth-century their outlook had become far less austere. The chapel itself, irreverently nicknamed 'the Congo', was built in the Neo-Gothic style used for so many Victorian buildings—an imitation of the style of the great medieval cathedrals, even to the tall spire. If this seems an odd choice for a decidedly Protestant institution, it was no odder than the Neo-Gothic banks, schools and railway stations put up in the nineteenth-century. Inside, the chapel was light and spacious, with blue and green decorations and a large organ and loft with 'Worship the Lord in the beauty of holiness' round the arch in front of it.

Instead of hell-fire, the congregation was usually treated to a sermon more like a lecture—perhaps even too 'reasonable' and undogmatic for some of its hearers, since the ministers were university men, infected with the contemporary scepticism of educated opinion concerning the literal truth of every word in the Bible; whereas there were still many ordinary people who believed that Adam and Eve were real persons and that biologists and geologists must be making terrible mistakes in their pronouncements about the age of the earth and the evolution of man from 'lower' forms of life. However, Mrs Lawrence evidently enjoyed the intellectual atmosphere, and later she also joined the literary society started by Robert Reid, the Scottish minister appointed in 1898. Both the minister and the Sunday School superintendant, Mr Remington, seem to have preferred martial rather than mournful hymns—such as 'Abide with Me'—and Bert Lawrence never failed to be stirred by 'Sound the Battle-Cry' and 'Stand Up, Stand Up for Jesus'.

Mrs Lawrence cultivated the minister, and used to invite him to tea. But the genteel nature of the occasion was likely to be marred by the arrival of Arthur Lawrence from the pit, ready either to reproach the minister with his clean hands and exemption from toil, or to appeal for his pity with a description of the collier's hard life. Both, naturally, embarrassed the minister and made Mrs Lawrence furious. Apart from any other consideration, the minister was the most highly placed social contact she could hope to make in Eastwood, ranking only below the mine-owners, the bank manager and a few other professional men, and the Anglican parson. And in fact, years later, Reid's recommendation did help to persuade the British School (next door to the 'Congo') to take on Bert Lawrence as a pupil-teacher.

Most Sundays ended quietly, with preparations for the working week. Not much changed from year to year in the lives of Mr and Mrs Lawrence: the passing of time was registered above all in the growth of the children and their gradual dispersion.

Growing up

Early childhood in Eastwood must have been quite exciting. There were the shops and squares and claypits of the town; the black-faced miners climbing up the hill from the pit; and the colliery itself, with shooting steam and clanking trucks of coal, gradually fading away until, after dark, nothing was left but a pattern of lights down the valley. And there was the countryside, stretching out in a vista of lanes, paths, hedges and fields from Beauvale Brook, only a short way from the Breach.

The Lawrence children got to know the countryside well, for they regularly walked across the fields to visit their grandparents in Brinsley. These were Arthur Lawrence's father and mother, John and Sarah Lawrence. John was a tailor who was largely—perhaps exclusively—employed by Barber, Walker & Co.; until the 1890s the company supplied all the colliers' pit clothes, so there was regular work for the old man. Great rolls of material, stacked up in the workshop, were a familiar sight to the Lawrence children—especially flannel, used for singlets and as lining for pit-trousers; and there was a big, strange-looking old sewing machine used in making the tough, heavy trousers. Some time in the 'nineties John Lawrence retired to a little cottage near the pit; the children continued to visit him there, and also saw three sets of aunts and uncles on the Lawrence side of the family, all held at Brinsley in the grip of the mine.

There was plenty to do closer to home. Naturally, forbidden places in the town exercised a fatal attraction. One such was the clay pits, ruled by a mysterious character the children called Mako Koko, who made and handed out a kind of toffee that they were half-afraid might poison them.

But in summer the brook called: there were places in it where you could swim, and just across the sheep-bridge you could see the sheep being sheared, or veer towards the pavilion of the cricket field which the colliery company provided for their men. A favourite game was to crawl under the pavilion, which was raised a foot or so above the ground on wooden blocks. The boys who were brave enough to crawl the length of the pavilion were hailed as good potential colliers by

Bathing in the brook

their friends, for most Eastwood boys thought it would be the finest thing in the world to follow their fathers' occupations.

Mrs Lawrence thought otherwise. In the ordinary course of things, her sons would have gone down the pit and her daughters into domestic service, at least until they got married. But, having been disappointed in her own life, Mrs Lawrence was determined to do better than that for her children. Like other ambitious parents she visualized them in 'white-collar' jobs which never involved getting dirty, such as clerking, teaching, or even (aspiring very high) the Congregationalist ministry. This was not just a matter of social prejudice: a clerk might not always earn as much as some manual workers, but he could hope for promotion and was less likely to find himself unemployed; and he did not share the manual worker's fear that his earnings would fall drastically as his physical strength declined with middle and old age. Even Mr Lawrence must have realized something of this, since although he resented the implied slight on mining, he never seriously opposed Mrs Lawrence's plans.

One advantage Mrs Lawrence gave her children was the ability to speak a standard, dialect-free English. Dialect had long since lost its romance for her, and she now saw it only as a sign of 'commonness', telling all the world its user belonged to the 'lower classes'. Her husband's insults when they quarrelled—calling her a 'sliving bitch' or telling her to 'hoad the faece' (shut up)—understandably strengthened her convictions. She used to claim that she had never been able to learn or even imitate the local mode of speech, but the way she brought up her children revealed her real attitude: they were never allowed to use dialect within her hearing, with the result that they actually grew up 'bi-lingual', since they employed dialect freely outside the house.

Most people now would find Mrs Lawrence's attitudes repellant— and the more so because she looked down on the colliers' ways not from a suburban villa but from the inside, as no more than a collier's wife with delusions of grandeur. If anything, we nowadays make a cult of dialect, prizing its rich vocabulary and unfamiliar harmonies. But in her own terms Mrs Lawrence was right: if her children were to 'get on'—to make even the slightest impression on the white-collar world—they would have to command a more widely understood idiom than broad Derbyshire.

Mrs Lawrence was only able to make plans for them at all because there were now greater opportunities for working-class children.

Arthur Lawrence had done well enough to become barely literate as a result of attending a few classes held by a Miss Eite at Brinsley; his children were given several years' education by order of the state and at its expense. The Education Act of 1870 made a real division between two generations of Eastwood families, just as it made a division between generations all over the country. The Act laid down that every child must have an 'elementary' education, and that where this was not provided by voluntary (mainly religious) schools, elected school boards should supervise the building of new 'board schools'. And within a few years further legislation made elementary education up to about the age of twelve both universal and free.

Beauvale Board School, set up in 1878 on the eastern edge of the town, educated all the Lawrence children, opening up new possibilities for them. Ernest, the Lawrences' second son, was a splendid scholar—so much so that even years later the headmaster held him up as an example to his youngest brother and sister. In fact Ernest was one of those marvellously gifted young people who so often seem to burn themselves out or die young. He had almost every imaginable good quality: he was clever, popular and athletic, and so full of vitality that he always leapt a fence rather than climb over it or go through a gate. He was good company, with a jocular nickname for every member of the family (Emily was 'Injun Topknot' because of her hairstyle, Bert 'Billy White-Nob') and a fund of boisterous humour; on one occasion, when Bert and Ada were dolefully burying a dead rabbit, Ernest suddenly appeared in a black silk hat with mourning streamers, lamenting with such noisy insincerity that the children's distress dissolved in laughter.

As if all this was not enough, Ernest was intensely ambitious and hard-working. He left school at twelve and held a series of clerical jobs while he learned shorthand and typing at evening classes; later still he took correspondence courses in Business French and German. His progress was so good that, when he was still only twenty-one, he was offered a job in the office of a London shipping underwriter. To understand what this meant to a boy from a little mining town, we have to remember that the City of London was then the financial capital of the world. And his employers, John Holroyd & Co. of Lime Street, were in the same line of business as the famous Lloyd's. It was a magnificent opportunity for Ernest.

Mrs Lawrence was torn between pride and possessiveness, and only let Ernest go with a certain bitterness: she wanted her children to be successes, but somehow to manage it while staying by her side. Her relations with her sons Ernest and Bert were particularly intense, almost lover-like; and they fully returned her feelings. She had frightened off the girls Ernest met at dances when they came calling; and when he took a job at Coventry, Ernest had cycled dutifully home every weekend.

The relationship continued after Ernest left for London, but he began to show clear signs of growing up. As a bachelor earning the princely sum of thirty shillings a week, Ernest could afford to send money home to keep his mother in smart gloves and boots. But without Mrs Lawrence there to interfere, he soon became engaged to a pretty, well-bred girl—one of the new breed of female office workers. The girl, Gypsy Dennis, was a gay little creature who enjoyed party-going and was quite willing to let Ernest spend his hard-earned money on her—though it is impossible to say at this distance in time whether she was as shallow as the very biased Mrs Lawrence believed.

In spite of his new entanglement, Ernest remained the family favourite, and he was received with rapture whenever he visited Eastwood, bearing crystallized fruits and other exotic presents. Now he would sometimes parade up and down the main street in his frock coat and silk hat; the colliers sneered at him—and no doubt felt a twinge of envy too—but Ernest's family looked on in awe, accepting him as the very model of a gentleman. None of them doubted that he would make a great career for himself, or that he and no other was the genius of the family.

And certainly the oldest girl, Emily, gradually settled from being a tomboy into a placid, conventional young woman. But Bert, the youngest boy, had something of Ernest's intelligence, though he lacked many of his brother's other qualities. He had been delicate as a baby, and in the first winter of his life Mrs Lawrence confided to a friend whom she met on the street that she did not expect the sickly little mite in the pram to live. She was wrong, but Bert grew into a painfully thin little boy, weighing so little that his brother George could carry him across the fields for hours without effort. Bert remained weak-chested and utterly incapable of joining in rough street games or competitive sports, and most of his early boyhood was spent in the company of girls. He was shy and over-sensitive too, but (in the right company) full of life and fun. He brought a strange, passionate attention to everything he saw or did, and people noticed

44

his peculiarly fine, quick reaction to persons, plants and animals. Inevitably, Emily was a second mother to him, and the rest of the family spoiled him. And he was so obviously frail that most adults were kind to him, though a few rough but harmless remarks might be enough to persuade him that he was being tormented past all bearing. Strangely enough, he enjoyed doing household jobs, and by the time he was ten could often be found with a big apron draped round him, cleaning knives and forks, polishing the family's boots, scrubbing the floor, or even blackleading the kitchen range. These were unusual occupations for a boy (even a frail one), since everybody thought of them as women's work. In nineteenth-century England no man expected to do housework, even if he was unemployed—although no doubt there were (as there have always been) domineering wives who ruled the 'master' of the house.

Many boys were less tolerant of Bert Lawrence than grown-ups and girls. At the Board School he was looked on as a cissy—weak, a bit stuck-up, and odd (he preferred girls to boys, and did a good deal of painting). At one time boys used to chant

Dicky Dicky Denches
Plays with the wenches

when they saw him with the girls; but the rather feeble jibe doesn't seem to have upset him.

School work was more of a worry. Bert was clever, but not much interested in the dull rote learning drilled into the boys at the Board School; and studying gave him headaches. It was Mrs Lawrence who drove him on, sharing his tasks and probably encouraging him to be like his big brother Ernest, of whom Bert felt a sort of affectionate jealousy. The headmaster, W.W.Whitehead, also helped, though at their first encounter he had been outraged by Bert's stubborn refusal to answer to his first name, David; Whitehead seemed to take this as some kind of slight on the King David of the Bible. But he was a conscientious teacher, and once he realized Bert's ability he set about coaching him for one of the new county scholarships.

It says a good deal for Whitehead's school that this could have happened. The Board Schools had many faults. At their worst they were simply factories for breaking the spirit and turning out obedient, literate drudges. (Many more literate workers were needed in Britain's increasingly complicated industrial society.) Classes were very large, and it was by no means uncommon for several classes of sixty to occupy the same large room while each worked on a

45

different lesson. Discipline was harsh; at Beauvale Whitehead used the cane freely to compel the respect and attention of the unruly colliers' sons. But at least there was a kind of crude equality of opportunity, inspection to restrain abuses, and for some pupils a definite purpose: quite a different situation from that of the schools so often described by Dickens—the private or charitable academies of a few years before, in which tyranny and favouritism flourished unchecked.

In 1898 Bert Lawrence won his scholarship, worth twelve pounds a year for three years. He was the first Eastwood boy to do so, and now became one of the privileged minority in England who went on to receive a secondary education. (The first state legislation on the subject was not passed until 1902.) In September 1898, when he was just thirteen, he enrolled as a pupil at Nottingham High School, an ancient, highly respectable institution where the masters were university men and wore mortar boards, and where Bert had to wear the standard uniform of blue cap and knicker bockers.

It was a real sacrifice to send him there. The scholarship meant three more years of supporting Bert, and for Mrs Lawrence three more years of skimping and saving. The twelve pounds covered only part of the cost of Bert's clothing, train fares, dinners and books; Mrs Lawrence complained bitterly, and appeared to have doubts, but it was probably certain from the very beginning that she would let him go.

Nor was it easy for Bert himself. He had to leave home at seven in the morning, rush to catch a train to Nottingham's Victoria Station, and then climb a hill to the school, arriving towards the end of Assembly. And by the time he got back home it was seven in the evening. It would have been exhausting for a more robust boy, and not surprisingly Bert developed a little cough he never afterwards got rid of.

This may account for the way his career at the High School tailed off. For a time he was outstandingly good at French, German and Writing, and later on he won prizes for Mathematics; but by the final year his position was fifteenth out of a class of nineteen.

Mr and Mrs Lawrence must have wondered at this stage whether it had been worth the sacrifices. Bert had not even made any friends or useful contacts at school. As the only collier's son in a middle-class institution that tried to create a 'public school' atmosphere, he may have felt rather out of place; and on one occasion the parents of a

46

Nottingham High School

friend stopped the boys meeting when they discovered Bert's background. On the other hand Bert was already a noticeably well-behaved, well-spoken boy (thanks to his mother), so geography may have had more to do with his difficulties. The long daily journeys to and from Nottingham must have made out-of-school friendships hard to develop, and his strained constitution cannot have been a good basis for academic achievement.

It was now decided that Bert, having had the luxury of three extra years' education, should follow the same path as his brother Ernest and find employment as a clerk. When an advertisement appeared in the *Nottinghamshire Guardian,* offering a clerical position in a firm making surgical goods, Bert answered it. His application was mainly the work of Ernest Lawrence, who was home on a visit and knew all there was to know about business letters. Still, there is an element of posthumous comedy in the fact of a great writer (as Bert was to become) being solemnly directed to put down the banalities admired as good business style: 'Should you favour me with the appointment I would always endeavour to merit the confidence you place in me', and so on. But in this matter Ernest really did know best: Bert got the job and went to work for Haywood's of Castle Gate in Nottingham.

At last he too was making a contribution to the family budget: thirteen shillings a week. For this he worked six full days in every week, starting at eight in the morning and finishing at eight almost every night—after which he had a train journey and a three kilometre walk home. It was some compensation that the working day at Haywood's was a peaceful, leisurely affair. The main drawback was the factory girls—a rough lot who embarrassed the sensitive Bert by bombarding him with suggestive remarks, and on one occasion cornered him and tried to tear off his trousers.

But there he was, spending his day perched on a high stool, translating letters from foreign customers and copying orders into a big book. This, it must have seemed certain, was to be the kind of thing he would do for the rest of his working life.

Life at Walker Street

Meanwhile the Lawrences had left the Breach. In 1891 they moved further up the hill to Walker Street, from which they had a splendid view of the valley across the waste ground and clay-pits; but the exposed position of the house made it vulnerable to the cold north wind, and Bert Lawrence nicknamed it 'Bleak House', after the novel by Charles Dickens.

The new home was socially superior to the house in the Breach, if only because it had a bay window (a matter of considerable prestige in those days). It was probably no coincidence that Ernest had just left school and gone to work, so that he had become a contributor instead of a dependant. The difference was a vital one, and the best years for many working-class families were those in which the children were employed and bringing home money, before they married and set up homes of their own. In a sense, Mrs Lawrence had a straightforward economic grievance against Gypsy Dennis for diverting resources away from the family.

But of course Mrs Lawrence would have hated any girl who threatened her hold on her beloved sons; within a few years she was showing the same kind of hostility to Bert's girlfriends. And she did nothing to stop all the children taking her side in quarrels with Arthur Lawrence, whom they learned to hate and despise. As a young man, Bert loathed his father so intensely that Arthur Lawrence's presence in the room killed the life in him and left him in a state of malignant sulks. Years afterwards—when it was too late—Bert and Ada came to see that there were two sides to the quarrels, and that Mrs Lawrence had done wrong in turning them against their father.

Arthur Lawrence certainly seemed nothing like an ogre to outsiders. Many years later, one Eastwood acquaintance remarked that he was 'always a perfect gentleman'; and May Chambers, the girl who noted the ugly transformation in Bert, also wrote that, at the time, Arthur Lawrence was chatting with her in a completely normal

49

and amiable manner. He was even normal enough to be proud of his ladylike wife and his clever children who knew French—though, naturally, when they were ranged against him he would disparage the usefulness of both ladylike airs and book learning.

There were still times when the conflicts were forgotten. Arthur Lawrence was at his best when he was active, and the children enjoyed it when he was cobbling or mending. He would sit on the floor in front of the hearth, his legs crossed tailor-fashion (after all, he was the son of a tailor), and hammer away, sing, and send the children scampering about to fetch tools and materials. At times he would read aloud to Mrs Lawrence from the newspapers, stumbling over some of the words and being prompted by his impatient wife. And when the younger children were small he delighted them by bringing home from the fields a baby rabbit, soon christened Adolf. Mrs Lawrence finally expelled Adolf when his droppings became too much of a nuisance. She detested pets because they introduced an element of dirt and anarchy into her clean and orderly house, though she reluctantly put up with rabbits, rats and a terrier called Rex, left in her charge by her brother Herbert the publican. On this issue at least, Arthur Lawrence and his children were allies in the cause of anarchy.

But all too often Arthur was out the whole evening, and, when he got back, became involved in rows with his wife about drinking and the housekeeping money. The children could hear their voices raised even above the wind moaning in the old ash tree across the road from the house. Then they would lie awake, dreading to hear thuds and shrieks, and only able to feel secure when their father's footsteps sounded on the stairs, taking him up to bed. Mealtimes could be unpleasant as well. When Mr Lawrence poured his tea into a saucer, blew on it and sucked it up, there would be grimaces of distaste. Provoked, he would make a point of eating and drinking as noisily as possible, deliberately turning himself into the pig his wife and children believed him to be. And from time to time he would simply blow up and rage against the malice of his wife and the ingratitude of his children.

Reading about families like this, it is hard to understand how they could bear staying together—to which part of the answer is that they more or less had to: the family was an economic unit, as well as the unit of respectability. But life is not all quarrels, even in the unhappiest families; and people have an astonishing capacity to go on

The miners' club—the pub

from day to day, working and bearing things and not even thinking themselves especially unfortunate.

And over the years Mrs Lawrence's life, at any rate, became easier. Housekeeping was less of a struggle once the older children began to earn money. In the mid-'nineties Emily left school and stayed at home, helping about the house; and as soon as Bert and Ada were old enough to look after themselves, their mother had the time and energy to take up some of her old interests. She read more, becoming absorbed in novels for the first time in many years; characteristically, she loved Sir Walter Scott's historical novels, which provided a form of high-class escapism, with plenty of noble heroes and pure heroines.

Most of the books came from the Mechanics' Institute, a nondescript building just across the road from the Sun Inn; its library held a thousand books and was open to borrowers for two hours a week, on Thursday afternoons. There were such institutes in many industrial towns, representing yet another aspect of working-class self-help. The first president of the Eastwood Institute, opened in the 1860s, was Thomas Barber the mineowner—in this as in other respects a patron of the colliers. Among other benefactions, the Barbers built the colliers' houses and set up the gasworks that supplied their homes. The relationship was much more patriarchal than we should expect to find in the mid-Victorian period of harsh masters and cut-throat competition. By the 1890s the relationship was dissolving as the owners became more efficiency-conscious and the colliers more willing to organize and demand rights rather than accept favours. However, the era of great strikes was yet to come, and some of the traditional gestures were still made—including the distribution of oranges and shiny new pennies to the colliers' children at Lamb Close, where they queued up to receive them every Christmas.

Mrs Lawrence's liberation meant that she could now go to the Women's Guild every Monday night. The Guild was an offshoot of the Co-operative Society, and gave the wives of Eastwood an opportunity to write papers on various subjects and read them aloud to the members; later on Bert and Ada remembered the surprise and admiration they felt at seeing their mother pondering her subject and then writing fluently. The colliers rather resented this activity on the part of their womenfolk, dimly sensing that there was danger to male supremacy in any gathering of women to discuss 'ideas'. For a time

Mrs Lawrence acted as secretary of the Guild, a task that included organizing parties to visit local beauty spots such as Matlock in Derbyshire, for which they hired a brake (a sort of large open cart drawn by a horse).

There were other, even more lighthearted diversions for the family. Twice a year the whole town went to the local fairs. The first, in September, was the Hill Top Wakes, held at the eastern end of the town, outside the Three Tuns Inn; then, in November, there was the Statutes and Fair, held on the other side of Eastwood, just down from the market place. The merry-go-rounds, coconut shies, shooting galleries and games were much the same as they are in modern fairs; only the peepshows, and real or reported marvels such as bearded ladies, are no longer seen, having long since yielded before the marvels shown on films and television. There were no sparking electric devices like modern dodgems, and the carved horses' heads and other equipment would have been cruder but also jollier and less stereotyped than their twentieth-century equivalents. As it grew darker, the ground would be dramatically lit by naphtha (oil) flares for the customers, by then chiefly young men and women. The small boys would linger as long as they dared, though they had probably spent their twopences—halfpenny by halfpenny—by early afternoon. Many of the men would have retired to the pub, and Arthur Lawrence's favourite, the Three Tuns, would be so packed that Arthur might help to serve drinks in return for some beer and pocket money.

Also very popular were the strolling players, who often took in Eastwood on their tours. The best-known, Teddy Rayner's company, set up a big tent and in good times might stay for months, harrowing their audiences at twopence a head with famous melodramas such as *Sweeney Todd, the Demon Barber of Fleet Street* and *Maria Marten, or Murder in the Red Barn*. The style of acting would have been as gruesome and exaggerated as the plots and dialogue; and the same kind of treatment would have been meted out to more subtle plays like *Hamlet*.

When there were no professionals to entertain them, the more enterprising inhabitants of Eastwood put on 'penny readings' at the British School on Albert Street. These consisted of musical or comic turns by local people, culminating in one of the most popular of all Victorian entertainments—a dramatic reading in the style of Dickens. (Dickens was a master of the art, reading from his own works on a

Nottingham Fair

number of enormously popular but exhausting tours that did a good deal to shorten his life.)

So things went on at Eastwood. But now a London tragedy occurred that shook the whole Lawrence family.

New directions

At the beginning of October 1901 Ernest came home specially to see Goose Fair at Nottingham. As far as the city was concerned, this was the greatest event of the year, a hectic, noisy, thrilling celebration that filled up the market place and brought all traffic in the city to a standstill. Compared with this, the Eastwood wakes were small and peaceful, and even in London Ernest felt the pull of the Fair.

Ernest had not been feeling well for some time. He stayed at Eastwood, and then in Nottingham with his brother George, who went with him to Nottingham's Victoria Station to see him off. George was concerned about Ernest's bad cold and inflamed face, and advised his brother to see a doctor and go to bed for a few days. But, conscientious and ambitious as ever, Ernest showed up at the office next day, only to be sent home to his lodgings in South London. Two days later his landlady decided to check on him, and discovered him on the floor of his room, unconscious and obviously dreadfully ill. She telegraphed Ernest's mother, who rushed to London; but he never regained consciousness. The cause of his death was acute inflammation (erysipelas) complicated by pneumonia. He was twenty-three years old.

Mrs Lawrence, though stricken, had the strength of will to make all the necessary arrangements; Mr Lawrence came up to London (for only the second time in his life) but he was too dazed and bewildered to be much help. Ernest's body was taken to Eastwood and he was laid out in his coffin in the parlour of the Walker Street house; and on the fourteenth of October he was buried at the local cemetery.

Mrs Lawrence never completely recovered from the blow: even years later she could never quite enter into the spirit of the parties and dances arranged by her other children and their friends. Immediately after Ernest's death she was blankly indifferent to everything but her grief: she even ignored Bert, who seems to have been plunged deeper into misery by this than by his brother's death. But then he too caught pneumonia—an event that, given its timing, looks suspiciously like a desperate attention-getting gesture. Such

56

psychosomatic illnesses occur quite often in over-intense family situations, probably developing from genuine weak spots like Bert's chest.

Whatever the truth of the matter, Bert was in real enough danger. Mrs Lawrence was roused from her despair and nursed him heroically until he was on the road to recovery. He was sent to spend a month by the sea at Skegness, where Mrs Lawrence's sister kept a boarding house, and then came back to Eastwood to finish convalescing. The following spring and summer he paid many visits to the Haggs, the farm in the Greasley area where the Chambers family lived. Mrs Lawrence had become friendly with Mrs Chambers at the Congregationalist chapel some years before, and in the summer of 1901 she had finally got round to walking the five kilometres through country lanes that separated the farm from Eastwood. Bert had gone with her, but his work at Haywood's prevented him from seeing much of the Chamberses for a time. Now he virtually fell in love with the whole family, perhaps because the atmosphere of the Haggs was free from the griefs and tensions that permeated his own home. The Haggs was only a smallholding, and Edmund Chambers supplemented his income by delivering milk around Eastwood. While Bert was still weak, Mr Chambers used to pick him up on his round and drive him to the farm. Bert had a wonderful time there, discussing religion with Mr Chambers, entertaining Mrs Chambers and the five children with imitations and newly invented games, and helping out around the farm. And a little later, when he was stronger, he joined Mr Chambers and his two oldest sons in haymaking; for some time the boys were his closest friends. Mrs Lawrence may have rejoiced to see her son flourish in the country air, but she soon became rather jealous of Bert's impatience to dash off almost every day to what had become his second home.

There was now no question of Bert returning to Haywood's or taking up any kind of business career: he was to become a teacher. Months of leisure to read and think must have influenced him in the direction of a more intellectual pursuit, for teaching was no easy option. Bert would have to become a pupil-teacher, spending about half his time teaching and the other half being taught. This system was typically Victorian in ensuring that the training paid for itself in work done by the trainee. The starting salary for Bert was five pounds a year (less than two shillings a week), which meant that Mr and Mrs Lawrence would again have to support him.

57

Haymaking

Bert was accepted as a pupil-teacher at the British School on the recommendation of the Reverend Reid. As we have seen, the school itself was something of a cultural centre in Eastwood, and it was soon to offer evening classes in Commercial Arithmetic, Domestic Economy and other subjects. It was a peculiar structure in the Neo-Gothic style, built in two halves like two medieval chapels side by side. The medieval style was even kept up at the expense of lighting: each 'chapel' had three narrow windows overlooking the street, crowned by a high oriel window. Most striking of all in a completely red-brick area, beneath its slate roof the British School was pale yellow, built entirely of rough-hewn sandstone blocks.

Here Bert Lawrence came every day to work under the head teacher, George Holderness. It was often hard work: Bert was not good at maintaining discipline, and at the British School he had to teach classes of forty unruly boys—who were well aware that he was not a 'real' teacher but a miner's son, just as they were themselves. And working in the same room as several other classes must have destroyed any chance of doing more than teach by rote. But there were compensations: the hours were much shorter than at Haywood's, and Bert saved a couple of hours a day by working at a place so near his home.

The following year it was different. The 1902 Education Act changed the system, and Bert now had to attend a Pupil-Teacher Centre at Ilkeston, just south of Eastwood. This meant a train journey again in the morning, though only a short one: on pleasant days Bert and his friends often walked back to Eastwood through the fields. The friends must have been the nicest feature of the change of system: once all the young pupil-teachers from the Eastwood area went to the same centre, they inevitably got to know one another well and came to think of themselves as a group, half-humorously called 'the Pagans'.

Ada Lawrence and the younger of the Chambers girls, Jessie, also became members of the group, though they were a year behind Bert and attended the Pupil-Teacher Centre on different days from him. Bert had encouraged Jessie's ambition to be more than a farm girl, and may well have helped persuade her parents to let her train as a teacher. Over the next few years Bert and Jessie developed a strange, intense relationship. They talked over all their ideas and experiences, and read and discussed the same books, but there was no declared romantic attachment and no sex. In those days such a relationship was difficult to keep up between unmarried people of opposite sexes: people—including those involved—generally expected it to advance (to romance, sex or marriage) or to fizzle out. It was hardest on the woman, brought up to think of mating or marrying as her chief goals in life, and at times Jessie wanted to stop seeing Bert; but he always dissuaded her. It is impossible now to know how sexually attracted to each other they were. Probably they did not know themselves: in a 'purity'-obsessed society it was hard for people to recognize how they felt and what they wanted, as distinct from how they were supposed to feel and what they ought to want. It seems likely that Jessie would have married Bert had he been willing. Bert, on the other hand, was not eager to lose his freedom—and a poor schoolteacher with a large family (usually unavoidable) really did lose his freedom. And there was another obstacle: Mrs Lawrence disliked Jessie, as she would have disliked any girl who threatened to replace her. For Bert, even more strongly tied to his mother than Ernest had been, it was in insuperable objection.

Mrs Lawrence never really liked the Walker Street house after Ernest's death, and the family soon moved round the corner to Lynn Croft Road. This was another step up socially, for the new home was semi-detached—which was as close to the suburban middle-class ideal as you could get in Eastwood. It also had many 'extras', such as a little entrance hall, two kitchen ranges (one in the scullery), and a china closet. The whole family was proud of it.

Perhaps that helped to make the family home a more lively place. Bert and Ada were now more or less grown up, and their friends were often at the house. Mrs Lawrence allowed girls to come and go as they pleased, laconically remarking that there was safety in numbers; she probably hoped they would counterbalance the influence of Jessie Chambers. On at least one occasion the young Lawrences held a Christmas Eve dance in the garret of the Lynn Croft Road house. Chinese lanterns were lit, and Bert made sure the floors were waxed, shredding some candles and then sliding about to work them into the floorboards. Then Bert, Ada and their friends danced to the fiddle. There were alarms when the lanterns caught fire, and even greater alarms when Bert took the party down to the parlour and thoroughly frightened them all with a ghost story, aided by a noisy intervention from his friend George Neville.

A few years later, Bert and the other Pagans began to visit William

Hopkin's house regularly on Sunday nights. Hopkin was a remarkable man who began life as a colliery clerk and cobbler, and eventually became a local councillor and magistrate. He became a life-long friend of Bert's, and in these early years of the century his house was the centre of 'progressive' thought in Eastwood. Hopkin's advocacy of socialism and the suffragette movement influenced many of the Pagans, and it was one emancipationist, the local chemist's wife, who gave Bert his first experience of sex. Altogether a meaningful first contact with the wider world and its preoccupations.

Some time before this, Bert's teaching career took a long step forward. Towards the end of 1904 he sat the King's Scholarship examination—and came out first in all England and Wales. This held out the prospect of a university education, and, as Bert thought, a dazzlingly different world of intellectual passion. But first Bert had to serve his last six months as a pupil-teacher and take the London Matriculation examination, which he passed in June 1905. Even then he could not go straight to college because he lacked the twenty pounds in advance fees, payable before he could enroll and collect his scholarship money. So he had to work a further year at the dreary British School while he and his family saved; and it evidently required a tremendous effort on the part of all of them, despite the fact that Emily had married and moved out the year before.

In September 1906 Bert entered Nottingham University College, a massive twenty-five-year-old Gothic edifice, grandiosely built of stone. At first he intended to read for a degree, but he soon switched to the Teacher's Cetificate course, which only took two years and did not require him to study Latin. The fact is that Bert quickly became utterly disillusioned: rightly or wrongly, he thought that the lecturers, so far from being intellectually passionate, merely went through the motions. He loathed teaching practice, mainly because he had to work under a master who trained boys to turn out stereotyped, lifelessly 'correct' work without the slightest creativity. And, being older than most of the students (twenty-one), he resented being treated 'like a kid'. But he stuck it out: he needed his paper qualification too badly to go in for gestures of protest.

In June 1908 Bert was awarded a Teacher's Certificate, First Class. However unsatisfying, college had meant leisure to read and write: now he must begin a career in earnest.

Departures

Bert's first job took him right away from home for the first time. This was semi-deliberate, since he decided he would not accept less than ninety pounds a year salary—not a vast sum, but ambitious for a man of Bert's age in a poorly paid profession. His friend Louie Burrows (a Derbyshire girl to whom he was later engaged for a time) found a job straight away—at seventy-five pounds a year. Bert expected more after all his years of training, and was perhaps also giving life a chance to tear him away from Eastwood, with its intense family life and network of difficult relationships.

His obstinacy was rewarded: at the last moment, when the autumn term had already begun, he was offered a job at ninety-five pounds a year, and left to work at the Davidson Road School in Croydon, just south of London.

And so the family shrank a little more, though the children frequently visited their parents, and both generations maintained contact with relatives scattered over the East Midlands. Now there were holidays away from home as well. This was still a very recent feature of working-class life, and one made possible by the development of the railways and cheap excursion fares from the 1870s. Until the late nineteenth century most inland families had never even seen the sea: Bert did so for the first time when he went to Skegness to recuperate, and not long afterwards he insisted on taking Ada and the Chambers family there on a day trip, so that they could share the wonderful experience of light and vastness. Slices of melon, unknown in Eastwood, completed the experience, though they were too hard and tasteless to be enjoyed for their own sakes.

Mr and Mrs Lawrence seem to have had their first seaside holiday in 1906, at Mablethorpe (like Skegness, on the Lincolnshire coast). They made up a party of relatives and friends that included Bert and Jessie Chambers; aside from other considerations, travelling as a party was cheaper. In subsequent years they went to Robin Hood's Bay and Flamborough, on the Yorkshire coast; and then in 1909 Bert—now in Croydon—went with his mother and some of the Pagans to Shanklin in the Isle of Wight. We could hardly have more graphic glimpses of achieved social change than these—of Nottinghamshire mining folk watching Cowes Regatta and the naval review in honour of George V and the Russian Tsar.

Next year, in August, Mrs Lawrence fell ill while on a visit to her sister in Leicester. She had to be brought home in a hired car, and Bert rushed to her side. The illness was cancer, and Mrs Lawrence took four months to die. Bert, numb with grief, managed to come home from his Croydon job one weekend in every two, nursing his mother devotedly and soothing himself while she slept by sitting painting beside her bed. By October she was 'horribly ill', and Bert's writer's eye noticed every detail of her face as it fell in. He was becoming known as a writer now, and he begged his publisher to hurry production of his first novel, *The White Peacock*, so that he could put a copy in his mother's hands before she died. It was done in time, but Mrs Lawrence was either past caring or unwilling to accept an independent achievement by her son. She looked at the book for a few moments and then it was put away.

Mrs Lawrence's death occurred in December 1910. That was virtually the end of the family unit, and so makes the proper place to end the story. Ada and Mr Lawrence left Lynn Croft a few months later, living for a time in lodgings; then Mr Lawrence went to live with Emily and her husband in Queen's Square, just below the Nottingham Road. Later, when they decided to move to Scotland, the old man rejoined Ada—now Mrs Clarke—at her home in Ripley, a mining town just across the border with Derbyshire. Finally Arthur Lawrence returned to Eastwood, living in lodgings at Bailey Grove until his death in 1924.

And so the family split up, though not in any tragic sense: the Lawrence children simply went their ways to start new families, as was in the order of things. Their lives, and particularly the life of Bert, who eloped with a married woman and blossomed into the famous and notorious D.H.Lawrence, would make a new and different set of stories.